MW00879282

African Baby
Names

SIMON STARR

ISBN 978-1533381514

PUBLISHED BY THE HOUSE OF STARR

PREFACE

"To speak the names of ones ancestors is to ensure they live eternally."

- Maxim of Kemet

Simon Starr

DEDICATION

This book is dedicated to the parents that strive to ensure their offspring know who and what they come from in order to best determine how they will turn out.

CONTENTS

Introduction

Simon Starr

Introduction

One compiled this book of baby names in order to help the descendants of the wondrous continent of Africa to reconnect with their native ancestral heritage and traditions.

Africa is not only the birthplace of humanity but also of complex customs, oral traditions and diverse peoples. The continent is home to several language families and hundreds of languages. The people can be divided into over a thousand different ethnic groups. Traditional African given names often reflect the circumstances at the time of birth. Names such as Mwanajuma "Friday", Esi "Sunday", Khamisi "Thursday", and Wekesa "harvest time" refer to the time or day when the child was born. Other names reflect the birth order of the newborn, for example Mosi "first born", Kunto "third born", Nsonowa "seventh born", and Wasswa "first of twins".

In order reflect the diversity of this magnificent continent, one has compiled names from the land of ancient Kemet (Egypt), Zulu peoples, Youroba peoples, Swahili peoples and Ethiopia (Amharic).

Simon Starr

Kemetian (Ancient Egyptian) Baby Names

Female -

A

AMENIRDIS…She Was Given by Amun

ANEKSI…She Belongs To Me

ASHAYT…She Who Possesses Abundance

B

BENERIB…Sweet of Heart

BENRET…Sweet One

H

HATSHEPSUT…Foremost of Noblewomen

HEBENY…Ebony

HEDJET…Splendid

HEMETRE…Servant of Re

HENUT…Mistress

HERUBEN…Resplendent Sky

HESETRE…Favored by Re

HETEPENAMEN…Peace of Amun

HETEPET…Peaceful

I

ISET/ASET…Original form of Isis

IYNEFERTI…Here Comes The Beauty

K

KAMAAT…Soul of Truth

KHUIT…Protected

M

MAATKARE…Truth is the Soul of Re

MERIT…Beloved One

MERITAMEN…Beloved of Amun

MERITATEN…Beloved of Aten

MERITITES…Beloved of her Father

MERITNETER…Beloved of the God

N

NEBET…Lady

NEBETAH…Lady of the Palace

NEBETNOFRET…Beautiful Lady

NEDJMET…Lovely

NEFERAMEN…Amun Is Good/Beautiful

NEFERTITI…The Beautiful Woman Has Come

NEFERTKAU…Beauty of Souls

NEFERTNESUT…Beautiful One of the King

NEFERUSHERY…Little Beauty

NOFRET…Beautiful Woman

NUBNOFRET…Gold and Beautiful

$\mathcal{R}$

RENPETNOFRET…Young and Beautiful

$\mathcal{S}$

SATDJEHUTI…Daughter of Djehuti

SENETNEDJMET…Lovely Sister

SHEPENSOPDET…A Gift From The Star Sirius

SHEPSET…Holy One

SHEPSETKAU…Holiness of Souls

SHERIT…Little One

$\mathcal{T}$

TAUSERT…Strong One

TENRE...She Who Belongs To Re

W

WERET...Great One

WIYA...Divine Bark

Y

YABET...Eastern Woman

YARET...Cobra Goddess

Kemetian Baby Names

MALE -

𝒜

AHA…Warrior

AHMOSE…Child of the Moon

AKHENATEN…He who is Useful to Aten

AKHENRE…He who is Useful to Re

AMENHOTEP…Amun is Pleased

AMENMOSE…Child of Amun

AMENNAKHT…Amun is Powerful

ℬ

BAKENAMEN…Servant of Amun

BAKENNEBEF…Servant of His Lord

BAKENPTAH…Servant of Ptah

BAKENRE…Servant of Re

D

DJEDEFHOR…Horus Is His Strength

DJEDEFRE…Re Is His Strength

DJOSER…Holy

H

HAPIMEN…Hapi (the Nile) is Eternal

HESIRE…Favored by Re

HOR-AHA…Horus the Warrior

HOREMAKHET…Horus on the Horizon

HOREMHEB…Horus on Jubilee

HORHERKHOPSEF…Horus Protects Him

HORHOTEP…Horus is Pleased

HORNAKHT…Horus is Powerful

I

IMHOTEP…In Peace

ITAMUN…Amun is the Father

ITNEDJEM…Good Father

K

KANEFER…Good of Soul

KAPTAH…Soul of Ptah

KAWAB…Pure of Soul

KHAEMWASET…Born in Waset (Thebes)

M

MEKETRE…Behold Re or Protected by Re

MEN…Eternal

MERENPTAH…Beloved of Ptah

MERIAMEN…Beloved of Amun

MERIATEN…Beloved of Aten

MERIATUM…Beloved of Atum

MERIRE…Beloved of Re

MERYIBRE…Beloved of the Heart of Re

MINMOSE…Child of Min

MINNAKHT…Min is Strong

N

NAKHT…Powerful

NAKHTMIN…Powerful is Min

NAKHTPAATEN…Powerful is the Aten

NEBAMEN…Amun is the Lord

NEFER…Beauty or Goodness

NEFEREFRE…His Beauty is Re

NEFERHOTEP…Peace is Good

NEFERMAAT…Truth is Good

NEHESY…Nubian

NESIAMEN…He Belongs to Amun

NESPTAH…He Belongs to Ptah

NETJERIKHET…Divine Body

P

PABEKAMEN…The Servant of Amun

PANEB…The Lord

PARAMESSE…Son of the Re

PASEBAKHAEMNIUT…Shining Star Above the City

PASHEDU…Shining

PENAMEN…He Who Belongs to Amun

PEPYNAKHT…Pepy is Strong

PIANKHI…The Living One

PINEDJEM…The Lovely One

PTAHHOTEP…Ptah is Pleased

PTAHMOSE…Child of Ptah

PTAHSHEPSES…Ptah is Majestic

R

RAHOTEP…Re is Pleased

RAMESSES…Child of Re

RAMOSE…Child of Re

RANEFER…Re is Beautiful

RAUSER...Re is Strong

RAWER...Re is Great

S

SEKHEM...Strong

SEKHEMKHET...Strong of Body

SENNEDJEM...Lovely Brother

SENNEFER...Good Brother

SENUSERT...Brother of Usert

SETEPENAMUN...Chosen of Amun

SETEPENRE...Chosen of Re

SETHEMWEYA...Seth in the Divine Bark

SETHI...He Belongs to Seth

SETHNAKHT...Seth is Powerful

SHEPSESKAF...Holy of Soul

SHEPSESKARE...Holy is the Soul of Re

SIAMUN...Son of Amun

SIATUM...Son of Atum

T

THUTMOSE…Child of Thot

TUTANKHAMEN…Living Image of Amun

TUTANKHATEN…Living Image of Aten

U

USERAMEN…Amun is Strong

USERKAF…Strong of Soul

Youroba Baby Names

𝒜

Aarin…Refers to centre/middle

Aarinade…In the centre of the crown

Aarinola…The centre of wealth

Abayomi…The enemy would have gloated over me

Abiola/Abimbola/Abisola…One born into wealth

Adebajo…The crown returns from a trip

Adeiye…The crown of salvation

Adekemi…The crown pampers me

Adelani…We own the crown

Adelanwa…It is a crown that we look for

Aremu…Is the name given to the first male child

Ariyo…One who is joy to behold

Ayo…Means joy

Ayotola…Joy is the worth of wealth

B

Baba…Father or grandfather

Babajide…Father has awoken

Babalola…Father is wealth

Babasola…Father makes wealth

Babatola…Father is the worth of wealth

Babatunde…Father has come again

Babatunji…Father had arisen/reincarnated

Babawale…Father has come home

Bolajoko…One who sits with wealth

Bolatito…So wealth is this big?

Bolutife…It is as God desires

D

Dideolu…The rising of God

Durodola…Wait for wealth

Durojaiye…Wait to enjoy (eat) life

Durosinmi…Wait to bury me

E

Ebunoluwa…Gift of God

Emiola…The spirit of wealth

Eni…Means person

Enilo…The person who went away

Eniola…Person of wealth

Enita…A person about whose birth a story is told

Ekundayo…Tears have become joy

Ereola…The benefit/advantage of wealth

Erioluwa…Evidence/testimony of God

Etoade…Right of the crown

Ewaoluwa…Beauty of God

Eyitola…This (one) is the worth of wealth

F

Faramade…Move closer to the crown

Fadekemi…Make use if the crown to pamper me

Fehintiola…Rest/relax on wealth

Feyifoluwa…Give this (one) to God

Fiyinfoluwa…Give prestige to God

Folashade…Use wealth as a crown

Fowosade…Use money as a crown

G

Gbekelolu…Rest on God

Gbadewole…Enter a place with the crown

Gbolagunte…Ascend the throne with wealth

Gbolahan…Show off wealth

Gbowoade…Receive the crown

I

Ibidun….Child birth is sweet

Ibijoke…Family pampers together

Ibikunle…Birth (children) fill the house

Ibilola…Childbirth is wealth

Ife…Means love

Ifeade…Love of the crown

Ifejobi…Love gave birth together

Ifetayo…Love is the worth of joy

Ikeolu…The care of God

Ilesanmi…Home benefits me

Ipadeola…Assembly of wealth

Iremide…My fortune/benefit has arrived

Iwalewa…Good character is beautiful

Iya…Refers to mother/grandmother

Iyabo…Mother has come

Iyadunni…Mother is sweet to have

Iyiola…The prestige of wealth

J

Jejelaiyegba…Life should be treaded gently

Jejeolaoluwa…The wealth of God is gentle/restful

Jenrola…Let me find wealth

Jokotade…Sit with the crown

Jokotola…Sit with wealth

K

Kalejaye…Sit and eat (savor) life

Kikelomo…Children are destined for pampering

Kofoworola…He does not buy wealth with money

Kokumo…He/she will not die again

Kukoyi…Death rejects this (one)

M

Magbagbeoluwa…Do not forget God

Makanjuola…Do not be in a hurry to get wealthy

Malomo…Don't go away any more

Matanmi…Don't deceive me

Meraola…I did not buy wealth

Mobolaji…I awoke with wealth

Modupe…I give thanks

Mofaderera…I adorn my body with a crown

Mofolami…I breathe with wealth

Mogbolade…I bring wealth home?

Mojirayo…I awoke to see joy

Mojirola…I awoke to see wealth

Mokolade…I have brought wealth

Molayo…I have joy

Monilola…I have a share in wealth

Mopelola…I am complete in wealth

Morakinyo…I have found a warrior to rejoice over

Morayo…I see joy

Morolake…I have found wealth to pamper

Motilewa…I come from home

Motunrayo…I have once again seen joy

O

Obafemi…The king loves me

Obileye…Family has honor

Odunayo…Year of joy

Oladepo…Wealth arrives its rightful position

Olalere…Wealth has benefits

Olamide…My wealth has come

Olawale…Wealth come home

Olayemi…Wealth befits me

Oluwadamilare…God exonerates/acquits me

Oluwadamilola…God makes me wealthy

Omolabake…Child whom we shall pamper

Omolabi…It's a child we have given birth to

Omolayo…Children are (a source) joy

Onifede…Here comes the person of love

Oreolu…Favor of God

Owo…This refers to money

Oyin…Honey/refers also to sweetness

S

Segilade…Ornaments are crowns

Segilola…Ornaments are wealth

Similolaoluwa…Restfulness of the wealth of God

Sijuwola…Look in the direction of wealth

𝒯

Tanimola…Who knows the future

Taraoluwa…From Gods own body

Temidayo…My life has taken a turn for good

Temitayo…My case is worth joyfulness

Tirenioluwa…It is yours, Lord!

Tinuade…From within the crown

Titilola…Endless wealth

Titilayo…Endless joy

Tiwalade…Ours is the crown

Tiwalolu…Ours is God

Tiwatope…Our situation is worthy of thanks

Tolulore…Gift which belongs to God

Toluwalase…God's word is law

Toluwani…Gods belonging

Towobola…Dip your hand into wealth

W

Wura…Means gold

Wurade…Gold of the crown

Wuraola…Gold of wealth

Y

Yejide…Mother has awoken

Yetunde…Mother has returned again

Yewande…Mother looked for me

Simon Starr

Ethiopian (Amharic) Baby Names

Female –

$\mathcal{A}$

Abeba...Flower

Abrihet ...She had made it light

Adanech...She a rescued them

Adina...She has saved

Afework...Speaks of pleasing things

Alam...World

Alitash...May I not lose you

Amhara...The Amhara people

Ayana...Beautiful flower

$\mathcal{B}$

Bathsheba...Daughter of an oath

Bekele...She has grown

Belkis...The Queen of Sheba

Berhane…My light

Berta…People of Ethiopia and Sudan

C

Cheren…Town in Eritrea

D

Debre…Mountain; hill

Debtera…Priest who is in training

Desse…Town in the Eritrea region

Desta…Happy

Dilla…Town in southern Ethiopia

F

Falasha…Landless ones; Ethiopian Jews

Falashina…Language spoken by Falashas

Fana…Light

Fannah…fun

G

Genat…Heaven

H

Habesha…Of the Ethiopian highlands

Hagos…Happy

J

Jahzara…Beloved princess

Jazarah…Beloved princess

𝒦

Kayla…Ethnic group and their language

Kelile…Protected

Keren…Town in Eritrea

Kess…Priest of an Ethiopian church

Kifle…My class

ℒ

Lebna…Spirit; heart

Louama…Sleep well

Lishan…Award; medal

Louam…Sleep well

ℳ

Magdala…Central highland town

Maharene…Forgive us

Makda…Woman of Magdala

Makeda…Beautiful

Mandera…Ethiopian border town

Melesse…Eternal

Mengesha…Kingdom

N

Negasi…She will be crowned

Nishan…Award; medal

Nyala…Rare mountain goat

Q

Qwara…People of Ethiopia

R

Retta…Won

S

Seble…Autumn

Selam…Peaceful

Selamawit…She is peaceful

Senalat…Happy

Sheba…From the Queen of Sheba

Shinasha…People of Ethiopia

Sisay…Omen of good things

T

Teru…Good

Tsage…Happiness

Z

Zala…People of Ethiopia

Zauditu…She is the crown

Ethiopian (Amharic) Baby Names

Male -

𝒜

Abai…The Nile river

Abebe…He has flourished

Afework…Speaks of pleasing things

Aman…Peaceful

Assefa…Enlarge

Atoberhan…Sunny

Azmera…Harvest

ℬ

Bekele…He has grown

Benaim…Son of the right hand

Berhanu…Your light

Berhanua…His light

Berihun…Let him be our guide

Berta…Be strong; persevere

Bworo…People of Ethiopia

D

Daniachew…You will be judged

Dawit…Beloved

Demissie…Destructor

E

Eremias…God will uplift

Ezana…Fourth century Christian king

F

Fasilidas…Historic king of Ethiopia

Fethee…Judgment

G

Gabra…An offering

Gebereal…God is my strength

Gebre…An offering

H

Hackeem…Doctor

Haeran…Masculine; virile

Hagos…Happy

Hakeem…Doctor

I

Iskander…Defender of mankind

Iyasu…Christian emperor

J

Jima…Town in southwest Ethiopia

K

Kafa…Area in southwestern Ethiopia

Kaleb…Reference biblical Cain

Kelile…My brother; my protector

Kelyle…Protected

Kifle…My share

L

Lebna…Spirit; heart

Lema…Cultivated

Louam…Sleep well

M

Mamo…My friend or buddy

Mekonnen…Respected; elite

Melaku…The angel

Mengesha…Kingdom

Merille…A people of Ethiopia

Miruts…Has been chosen

N

Nazaret…Town named for Nazareth

Negash…Next in line for the throne

Negasi…He will be crowned

Negus…King or emperor

O

Ogbae…Don't take him away

Ogbai…Don't take him away

Ogbay…Don't take from me

Oromo…Large ethnic group; herdsmen

R

Rahad…River in Ethiopia

Ras…Leader; equivalent to duke

S

Selam…Peaceful

Selassie…Trinity

Semer…Farmer

Sisay…Omen of good things

T

Tamirat…Miracle

Tariku…Events surrounding his birth

Taye…He has been seen

Tefer…Seed

Teferi…Is feared

Teka…He has replaced

Tekle…My plant

Tengene…My protector

Teruworq…Good gold

Tesfaye…My hope

Tessema…He has been heard

Tewodros…Gift of God

y

Yacob…Substitute

Yohannas…God's gracious gift

Yonas…Dove

z

Zere…The descendent of

Zere Mamo…The descendent of Mamo

Zere Tesfaye…The descendent of Tesfaye

Zere Yacob…The descendent of Jacob

Zula…Port town in Eritrea

Simon Starr

Zulu Baby Names

Female -

A

Amahle…The beautiful ones

Andile…The family is growing

Ayize…Let it happen / come

B

Busisiwe…Blessed

D

Duduzile…Consoled

Dumisile…They have praised

G

Gugu…Precious/treasure

H

Hlengiwe…Redeemed

J

Jabulile…She is happy

K

Khanyisile…Bringer of light,brought light

Khethiwe…Chosen, the one who is chosen

L

Lindiwe…Waited for

M

Mbali…Flower

Minehle…Beautiful day

Msizi…Helper

N

Nandi…Sweet

Nkosingiphile…The Lord gave me

Nobuhle…The beautiful one

Nolwazi…The one with knowledge

Nomathemba…Hope

Nomsa…Short for Nomusa

Nomusa…With grace / kindness

Nomvula…After the rain

Nomzamo…Struggle

Nonhlanhla…Luck

Nonkululeko…Freedom

Nozipho…Giver of gifts

Ntokozo…Joy / happiness

Ntombifuthi…Another girl

Ntombizanele…Enough girls

Ntombizodwa…Only girls

Ntombizonke…All girls

S

Sibongile…We are thankful

Samukelisiwe…We have received e.g a gift.

Simangele…Surprise

Simosihle…Beautiful feeling

Sindisiwe…Saved

Sinethemba…We have hope

Sinenhlanhla…We have luck

Siphephelo…Refuge/ place of peace

Siphokazi…Gift

Slindile…We're waiting

T

Thabisa…Bring joy

Thandeka…Beloved

Thandiwe...Loved

Thembisile…Promised

Thenjiwe…The trusted one

Tholakele…Found

Thulisile…She who made things quiet

Z

Zinhle…The girls are good/beautiful

Zodwa…Short of Ntombizodwa

Zama…Try

Zandile…They have multiplied

Zulu Baby Names

Male -

A

Ayanda…They augment (the family)

B

Bandile…They have extended in number

Bheka…Behold

Bhekizizwe…Look after the nations

Bhekithemba…Look after hope / look for hope

Bonginkosi…Thank the Lord

Bongani…Be thankful

Buyisiwe…Returned

D

Dingane…One who is searching

Dingani…What do you need

Dumisani…Praise God

J

Jabulani…Rejoice

K

Kwanele…It is enough

L

Lwazi…The one with knowledge

Lindelani…Wait

Londisizwe…Protect / take care of the nation

M

Mandla…Power

Mandlenkosi…Power of God

Manelesi…Satisfier

Mlungisi…Fixer

Mondli…Feeder

Mthandeni…Love him/her

Muzikayise…He who builds his father's home

N

Nathi…Short for Nkosinathi

Nhlakanipho…Wisdom

Njabulo…Happiness

Nkosinathi…God is with us

Nkosiphendule…God has answered

P

Phila…In good health (be well)

Philani…Be well (plural)

Phumlani…Rest

S

Sakhile…We have built

Sandile…We have increased

Sanele…We are satified / have enough

Sibongiseni…Be thankful with us

Siboniso…Being a leader

Sibusiso…Blessing

Sifiso…Wish / what we had wished for

Simphiwe…We have been given him/her

Siphelele…We are complete

Sipho…Gift

Siphosethu…Our gift

Sithembiso…A promise

Siyabonga…We thank you

Siyanda…We are increasing

Sizwe…Nation

Siphamandla…Give us strength

T

Thabo…Happiness

Thalente…Talent

Thamsanqa…We have luck

Thando…Love

Themba…Trust, hope, faith

Thulani…Be still / quiet (used as a consolation, 'hush')

L

Lwazi…Knowledge

U

Unathi…She is with us

V

Vusumuzi…Builder of the home

W

Wandile…You are extra

X

Xolani…You all have peace

Z

Zithembe…Trust yoursel

Zonkizizwe…All nations

Ziphozonke…All the gifts

Simon Starr

Swahili Baby Names

Female -

A

Abbo…Vegetable

Adhama…Glory

Adia…A gift from God

Afiya…Health

 Aisha…Life; woman

Akina…Relations

Aleela…She cries

Aluna…Come here

Amana…To believe

Amanika…Trustworthy

Andaiye…Daughter comes home

Angalia…Alert and observant

Arusi…Born during a wedding

Ashante…Tribe in West Africa

Asya…Born during time of grief

Atiena…Guardian of the night

Ayah…Bright

Ayubu…Patience in suffering

$\mathcal{B}$

Bahati…Luck

Bakari…Noble promise

Baraka…Blessing; fortune

Barika…Success

Bavana…Clear knowledge

Bayinika…Manifest clarity

Budhya…Enlightened one

Busara…Practical wisdom

C

Chagina…Brave one

Chanua…Blossom

Chiku…Chatterer

Chinira…God receives

Chriki…Blessing

D

Dafina…Treasure

Dalia…Gentle

Dhamiria…Thoughtful aim

Dinka…A tribe of people

E

Elea…Floating; clear

Elewa…Understands

Elimisha…Teaches knowledge

Endana…To love unconditionally

Endelea…Becomes famous

F

Fanaka…Prospers and succeeds

Faraji…Consolation

Farijika…Console and help

Fatuma…Weaned

Fikira…With deep thoughts

G

Gethera…Harvest

Goma…Joyful dance

H

Hadiya…Present

Halima…Gift

Halina…Gentle

Halisi…Authentic; genuine

Haoniyao…Born during a quarrel

Hasana…She arrived first

Hasanati/Hasina…Good

Hawa…Longing

Heshima…Respect; honor

Himaya…Protection

Hodari…Strong; powerful

Huseina…She arrived first

I

Imani…Belief; trust

Imara…Strong one; resolute

Imarisha…Establish and stabilize

Inira…To sing

Inithia…Leads in song and dance

Issa…The Lord is my salvation

Itanya…Hope

J

Jaha…Dignity

Jahaira…Dignified

Jama…Friend

Jamaa…Kin; relation

Jamani…Friend

Jamba…A hero

Jehlani…Strong; mighty

Jiona…To glow with pride

Julisha…The advisor; gives advice

K

Kakena…The happy one

Kalere…Short woman

Kaluwa…Forgotten one

Kamara…Moonlight

Kamaria…Like the moon

Kanene…Important thing

Kanisa…A church

Karama…Honor

Kenithia…Happy; joyful one

Kenura…Joy

Kesi…Born during difficult times

Khadija…Born prematurely

Kiama…Magic

Kiania…The dawn

Kibibi…Little lady

Kichea…Brightness; the sun

Kiira…The dawn

Kijakazi…Your life is owed to us

Kilinda…Guard; protector

Kinaya…Independence

Kinjia…The path; the way

Kito…Precious stone

Koffi…Born on Friday

Kudio…Born on Monday

Kuende…Growth; evolution

Kwanzaa…Feast of first fruits

Kwashi…Born on Thursday

L

Lindana…The defender

Lindia…The defender

Lisha…To nourish and cherish

M

Madini…A gem

Mahiri…Skillful and clever

Majda…Glorious

Maji…Water

Majida…Honor; excellent glory

Malika…Angel

Maliza…Accomplishment

Malkia…Queen

Maridhia…Content; satisfied

Marijani…Coral

Marini…Healthy; pretty

Mashika…Born during rainy season

Masika…Born during rainy season

Maskini…Poor

Msia…Wise woman

Muraty…Friend

Mwamini…Honest

Mwanahamisi…Born on Thursday

Mwanaidi…Born during Idd festival

Mwasaa…Timely

Mwatabu…Born during sorrow

N

Nadira…Rare

Najuma…Abounding in joy

Nbushe…The godly one

Neema…Born during prosperous times

Nigesa…Born during harvest season

Nurisha…Give light; enlighten

Nyota…Star

O

Onyesha…Clear; sight

Otesha…Cultivate the earth

Oyana…Uplift & inspire

P

Panya…Mouse; tiny baby

Pasua…Born by cesarean section

Penda…Loved

R

Radhiya…Agreeable one

Rasheda…Rightly guided

Rashida…Rightly guided

Raziya…Agreeable

Rehema…Compassion

Risala…Messenger

Rukiya…She rises up

S

Saada…Help

Safika…To set right

Safiri…A journey

Salama…Peaceful one

Sanura…Kitten

Sauda…Beautiful and dark-skinned

Shani…Marvelous; wonderful

Shauri/Shauriana …Counsel; advise

Sikudhani…A surprise; unusual

Siti…Respected woman

Siwazuru…Not nice people; conflict

Subira…Patience

T

Taabu…Troubles

Tabara…Prosperity

Tajia…Crown

Tamu…Sweet & delightful

Therania…Bright shine

Tia…Respect

Tisa   Ninth-born

Tuliza   One who's calm

U

Ujamaa…Fellowship; brotherhood

Ujana…Youth

Umija…Unity; togetherness

Usia…Wisdom

W

Waseme…Let them talk

Winda…Hunter

Z

Zahra…Flower; white

Zaida…The better one

Zakia…Smart; chaste

Zakiya…Intelligent one

Zawadi …A gift; a present

Zuri…Beautiful

Zuwena…Good

Swahili Baby Names

Male -

$\mathcal{A}$

Abasi…Stern

Adhama…Glory

Amani…Trust; safety

Anasa…Joy

Ashon…Seventh-born son

Atieno…Guardian of the night

Ayo…Joy

Azima…Magically charmed into motion

Azizi…Precious

$\mathcal{B}$

Badru…Born during a full moon

Baraka…Blessing; fortune

Barasa…Meeting people

Bayana…Clear knowledge

Beno…One of a band

Busar…Practical wisdom

Busara…Sense; foresight

Bwana Mkubwa…Great master

C

Chilemba…Turban

Chitundu…Bird's nest

D

Darweshi…Saintly

Daudi…Beloved one

Duma…Cheetah

E

Elea…Floating; clarity

Elim…Knowledge

F

Fanaka…Success; valuable

Faraji…Consolation

Farijika…Console and help

H

Habib…Beloved

Hali…Authentic; genuine

Hamadi…Praised

Hamidi…Admired

Hamisi…Born on Thursday

Hanif…Believer

Haoniyao…Born during a quarrel

Hodari…Strong; powerful

I

Ikeno…Joy

Issa…God is our salvation

J

Jafari…Creek

Jamal…Handsome; beautiful

Jamba…A hero

Jata…Celestial star

Jela…Father suffers during wife's labor

Juma…Born on Friday

Jumaane…Born on Tuesday

K

Kamari…Moonlight

Keambiroiro…Mountain of blackness

Keanjaho…Mountain of beans

Halfani…Destined to rule

Kiama…Magic

Kifeda…Only boy born among sisters

Kiira…The dawn

Kito…Jewel; precious child

Kitwana…Pledged to live

Kobe…Turtle

Koman …The understanding one

Kuende…Growth; evolution

Kwanzaa…Feast of first fruits

M

Madaadi…Name of an age group

Mbita…Born on a cold night

Mhina…Delightful

Mosi…First-born child

Moyo…Heart

Mpenda…Lover; fond

Mshindi…Champion

Msia…Wise man

Mune…The rules

Muraty…Friend

Musa…Saved from the water

Mwinyi…One who summons

Mzuzi…Inventive

N

Neema…Born during prosperous times

Njowga…Shoes

Nyo…Star

O

Okapi…Related to the giraffe

S

Safiri…A journey

Salehe…Good

Sefu…Sword

Shani…Marvelous; wonderful

Shomari…Forceful

Simba…Lion; a strong person

T

Tabia…One of good character

Tajia…Crown

Tambo…Vigorous

Tamu…Sweet & delightful

Tian…Respect

U

Umoja…Unity; harmony

Usian…Wisdom

Y

Yahya…God's gift

Z

Zahur…Flower

Zakia…Intelligent

Zawadi…Gift

The End

Simon Starr

Also by Simon Starr

Jesus Christ - The Misunderstood
Messiah

The Road to Greatness

Enchanting Wisdom of Native Americans

Men Made Simple

Know Thy Self

Simon Starr

Made in United States
North Haven, CT
28 May 2023

37089409R00050